Small Sacrifices

The Making of a Tiny Epic

Small Sacrifices: The Making of a Tiny Epic
Neil Baker
ISBN: 978-1-257-95351-6

CONTENTS

The Concept

Initial Designs

Building a World

Small Stuff

The Cabin

Filming the Climb

Smoke and Mirrors

Computer Bugs

Soundscapes

Promotion

Credits

The Concept

Small Sacrifices began life as an idea for a short film treatment during an animation class at De Anza College in Cupertino, California. Neil Baker, a student there at the time, considered a story about the first conquest of Mount Everest by Edmund Hillary and Tenzing Norgay in 1953, but told from the perspective of a team of fleas that are attempting to scale Hillary's hat at the same time.

During a series of rewrites, it was quickly established that the human element was not needed at all, which would not only make production easier (no live-action to contend with) but could then use the insects as metaphors for mankind's whims and follies at the expense of others.

Reprinted here is the revised concept that would be the starting point of the film project.

> *The new storyline concerns the efforts of a team of flea Sherpas as they accompany a bloated, pompous louse in his efforts to conquer a snowy peak. There are five Sherpas in all, two scouts and three porters who are laden down with unnecessary equipment. They are all tethered together with the louse in the middle behind the two scouts. As the climb progresses, the team encounters many hazards along the way. The first casualty is one of the scouts who disappears down a hidden crevice. One of the porters is used to bridge the gap, and is left dangling there as the climbing party moves on. The first night on the mountain is bitterly cold, although the louse is perfectly comfortable in his tent and leather reading chair. Outside the fleas shiver. The next morning reveals another of the porters has frozen to death. The reduced party (the louse, one over-laden porter and one scout) continues the ascent and is nearing the summit when the louse makes a sudden noise, which causes a small avalanche, sweeping the last porter away (tethers are hastily cut during this). The remaining scout leads the louse to the summit, where he is pushed to one side so that the louse can claim the glory. He is forced to take several triumphant photographs of the louse even though he is on his last legs, then the scout finally gives up the ghost and flips over, close to death. The louse ponders his predicament for a second – how will he get down from the mountain? Then he looks at the dying flea. The final scene shows the louse riding the feeble flea scout down the mountainside at breakneck speed like a toboggan. They flash past the scenes of previous carnage, and over the flea still bridging the crevice, before arriving at the base to the flash of camera bulbs. The final image is of the louse, resplendent in his triumph, posing with one foot on the carcass of his flea scout.*

During the course of writing the outlines, it became apparent that the film needed a villain, and an appropriate creature was required to fit the bill. Neil ultimately settled on a louse, not only for the negative connotations of the word, but because of its ungainly structure and natural pomposity. The louse took on a decidedly European flavor, and Neil has admitted that he always had Gert Frobes from 'Goldfinger' at the back of his mind while he wrote this character.

While Neil revised his treatment drafts, he made constant sketches as he tried to establish a look for the characters in the film. Here are some of his early images, which would later influence the concept art during pre-production.

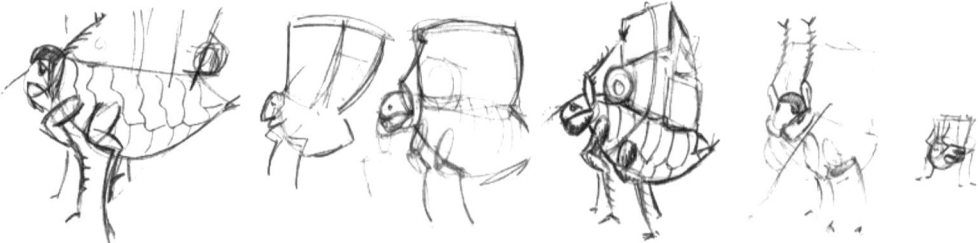

Initial Designs

While Neil finished post-production on his then current stop motion film, *The Cleaning*, he began to make rough sketches of the characters for his next film, and also drew out a few key scenes from the story.

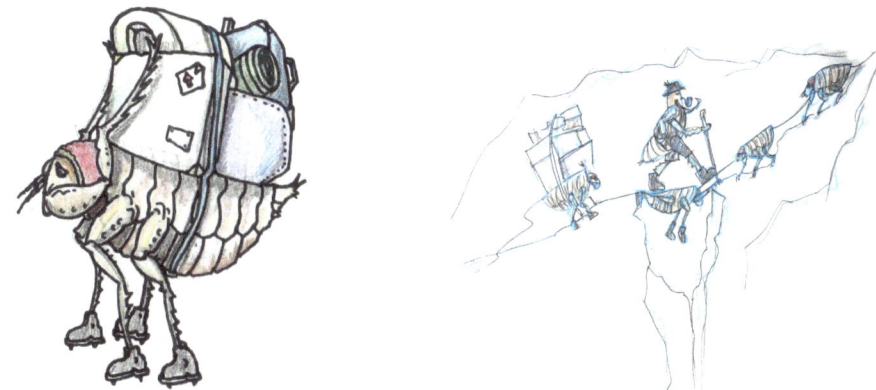

Neil's final 'Flea Sherpa' design. The arms extending from the flea's faces, though anatomically correct, would be changed later on due to the possible armature difficulties this would present and lack of head movement. Also above is a thumbnail sketch of the 'crevice' scene with the louse using a flea as a bridge. Below is a sketch of the triumphant louse at the summit, and an early design for 'Count Otto Von Louse' himself.

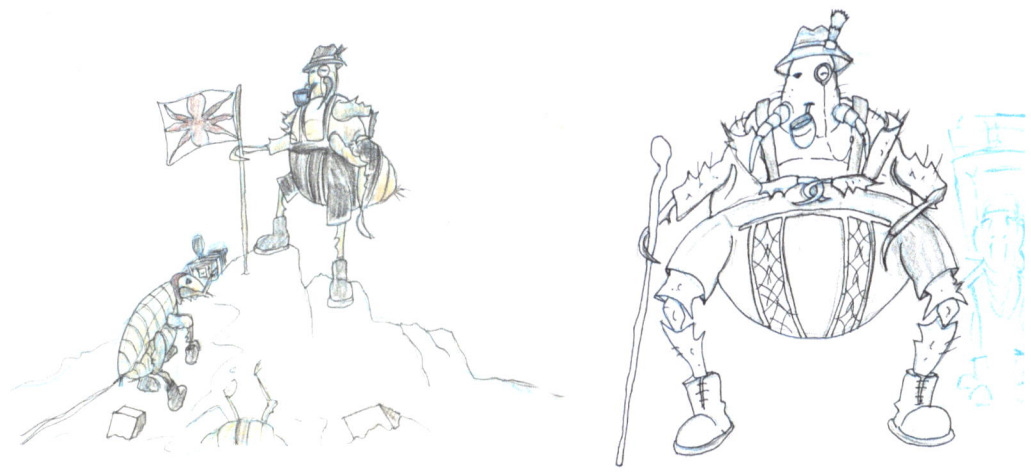

During the final phases of *The Cleaning*, Neil broached the subject of Small Sacrifices with his animators, and Keenan Manely jumped on board from the beginning. With a lead animator in place, Neil then turned to Phillip Vaughan, a fellow student who was known for his exquisite artwork. Phil was asked to create some concept images based on Neil's original sketches, and he delivered in spades.

Phil's early works explored the characters of the fleas and how to define them, and he included a turnaround of the Sherpa physique.

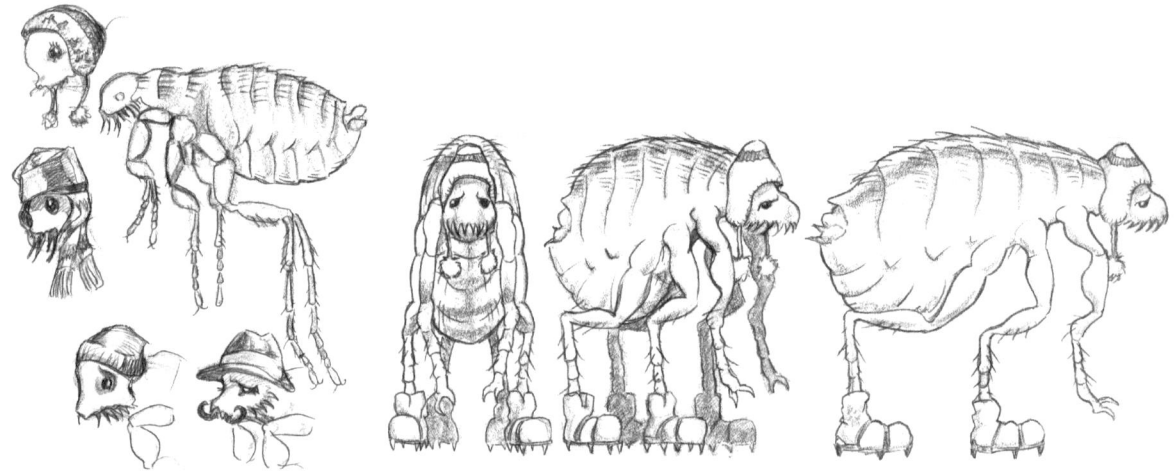

Phil's concept of the Louse was a major influence on his eventual personality, and Phil also recreated one of Neil's early scenes.

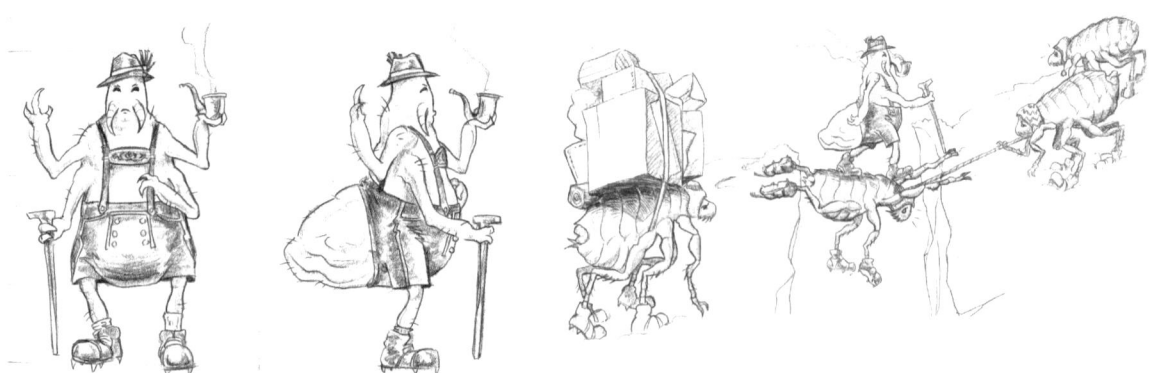

When it came to the mighty mountain (nicknamed *The Gnatterhorn*) itself, Neil had drawn a few crude ideas on the white board during crew meetings, but essentially his outline was to make it just shy of realistic-looking; fantastic enough to belong in this surreal story, but real enough to be recognizable to the audience with regard to its formidable dangers. Neil's final criterion was for it to look like a soft-serve ice cream, as if constantly in motion, more organic than a regular geometric mountain.

Phil turned in a plethora of mountain concepts, including the two shown below. He really captured the organic feel in the colorized version of his sketches.

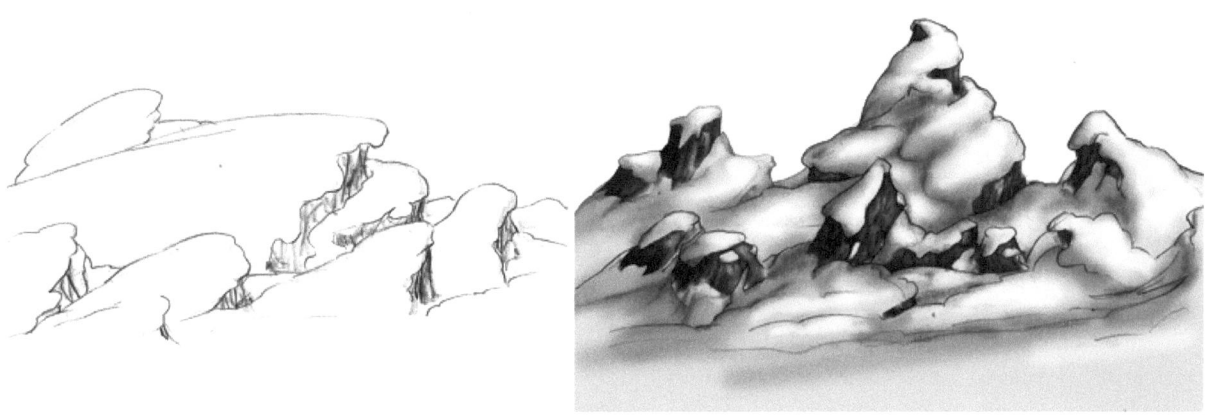

Keenan then went ahead and drew a sketch of the overall shape of the mountain. This was very close to what Neil had in mind, and so it became the basis for all subsequent digital models that would be used to augment the film in post-production.

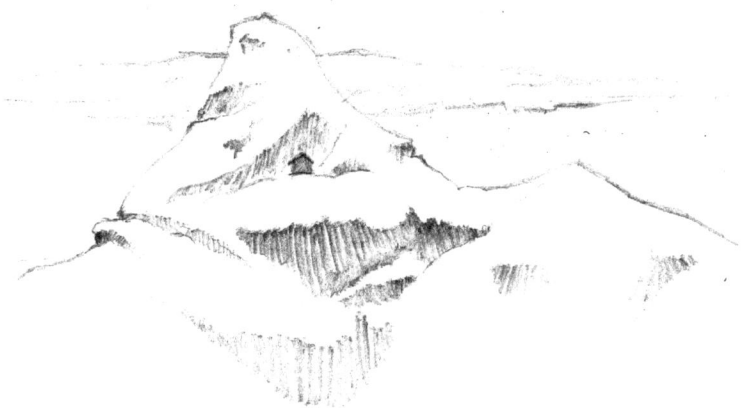

Many of the other sets and props were also sketched out by Neil and Phil, and one of the main designs would be the cabin.

Neil described his vision for the little wooden cabin that would be the insects' resting place for the night, citing the cabin in Chaplin's '*The Gold Rush*' as inspiration for the design. From this description, Phil turned in a few concept sketches.

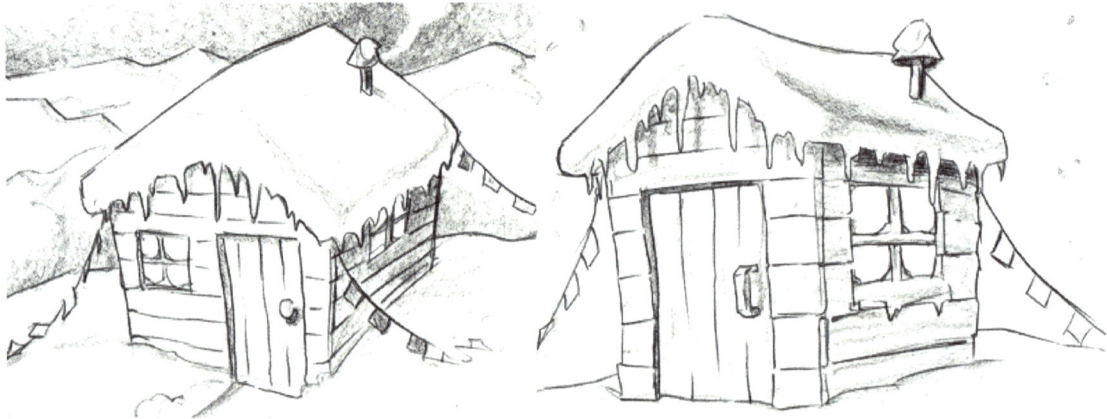

It was decided to go with the cabin with the window on the front, as this would serve the interior lighting set-up better. Next, George Parashis, who had been brought onboard for his model making and CG skills, supplied a series of basic computer simulations of the cabin, created using Carrara, which would serve as templates for the final model.

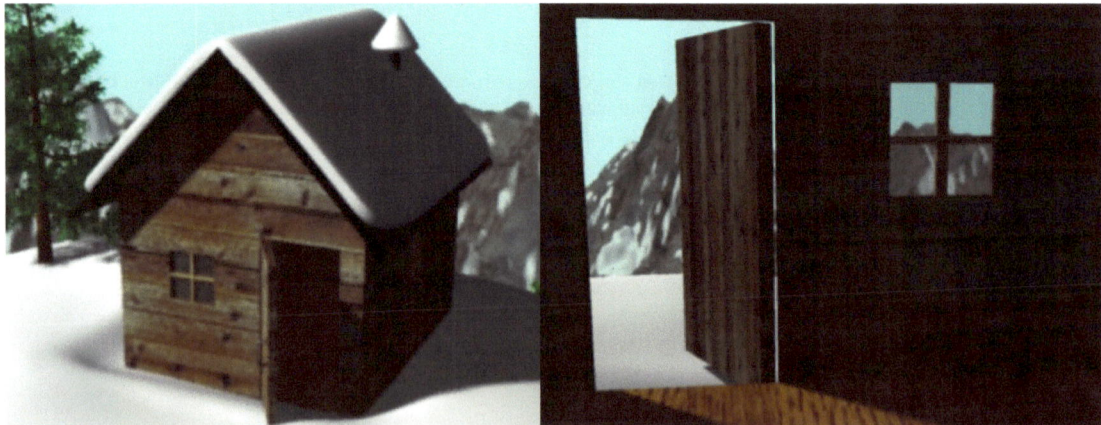

From these concepts, George was able to fashion a superbly detailed wooden cabin that would stand up to an intense shooting schedule over the course of the 30-month production.

All that was left to do was to start building everything…

Building a World

Many of the sets, puppets and props were built simultaneously as more and more artists and animators joined the crew.

As construction began on the main mountain set, Jacob Rossi, one of the animators from *The Cleaning*, and Roberta Home, who would later become Associate Producer amongst other roles, pitched in with Neil, Phil and Keenan to help build the mammoth set. Jon Oren, I.T. wiz, soon joined them and he was followed by a gaggle of friends as the mountain took shape.

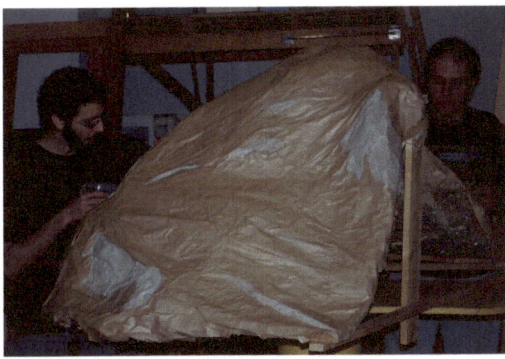 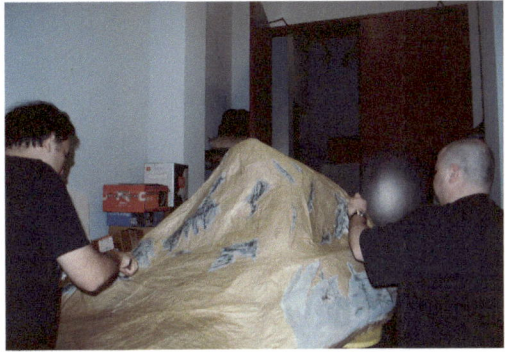

The mountain began as a wooden frame covered with chicken wire and paper maché, strengthened with a glue mixture.

Rock forms were created by stippling onto the wet paper surface, then painted and detailed using a dry brush technique.

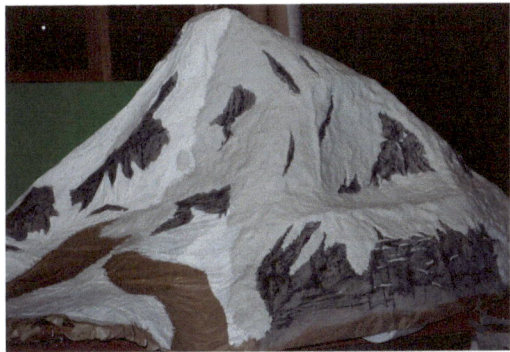 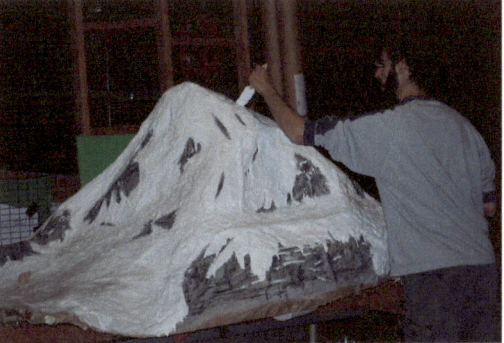

A thin layer of clay was used to further define the mountain, and then finally several coats of white paint infused with glue and baking powder were applied. Above you can see Jon applying the final coats to the summit of *The Gnatterhorn*.

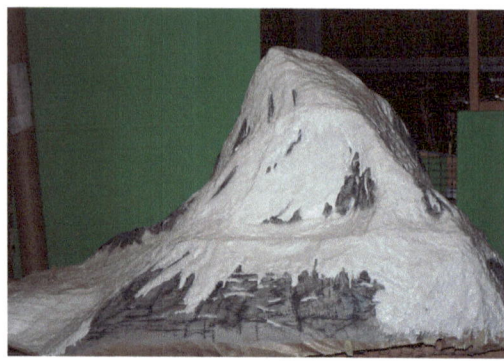 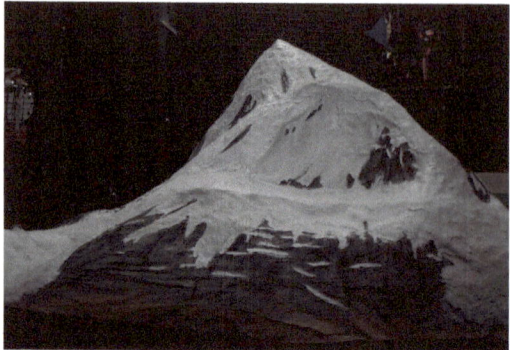

When the last of the paint/glue/powder layers was dry the mountain had a flowing quality to it, but was too reflective, so the crew liberally covered the surface with a thin layer of baking powder, which absorbed some of the light and created a nicely sparkling layer of 'snow' for the insects to walk through. In all, approximately 10lbs of baking powder was used during filming.

Using the same technique, three additional set pieces were created that could be used in a variety of ways, including rear rock faces, cliff faces, steep inclines and crevices. Below is a simple yet versatile set piece that was detailed to be used in capacity.

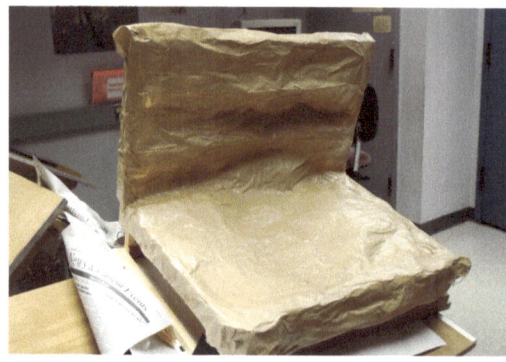 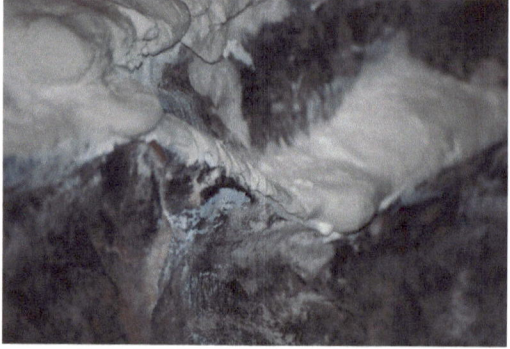

These sets were lightweight enough to able to clamp them in any position and, as you will observe later in the book, were used extensively for many of the scenes that did not take place on the summit itself. The paper maché/wire frame structure meant that puppet lockdown was simple. The insects all had holes in their boots into which screws could be tightened from beneath the set. Then, when the characters moved on, the holes could be filled with clay and baking powder.

With the sets in place, all that was needed were the actors, and so began the bug building…

In order to build the flea puppets, Neil began with a simple armature and clay maquette to determine the form and size of the insects.

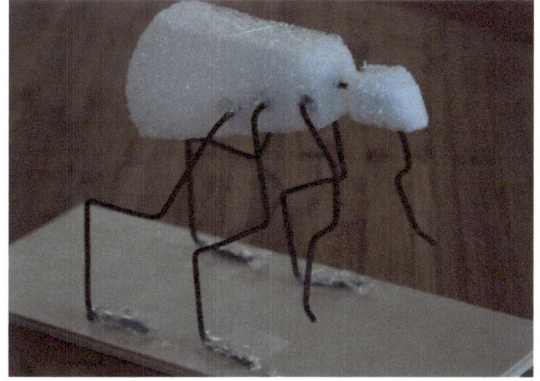 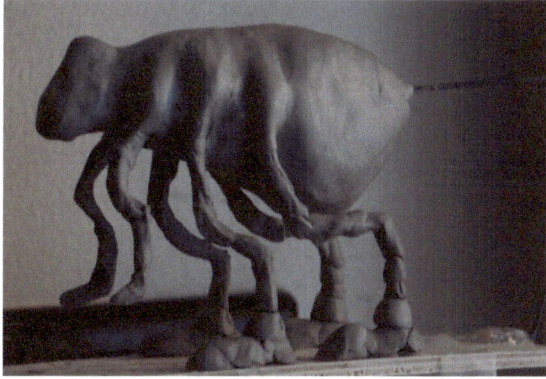

It was immediately evident that these would be too bulky, so Neil devised another solution. First, he took Phil's original flea concept drawing and divided it into 'segments'. He then sculpted over the segments in clay, and made a plaster mold of the pieces. Then, Neil used the negative forms as templates into which he pushed sculpy. When the sculpy hardened it could be glued onto the wire armatures and then augmented with latex and cotton wool. This resulted in a basic flea form that could then be adapted at whim.

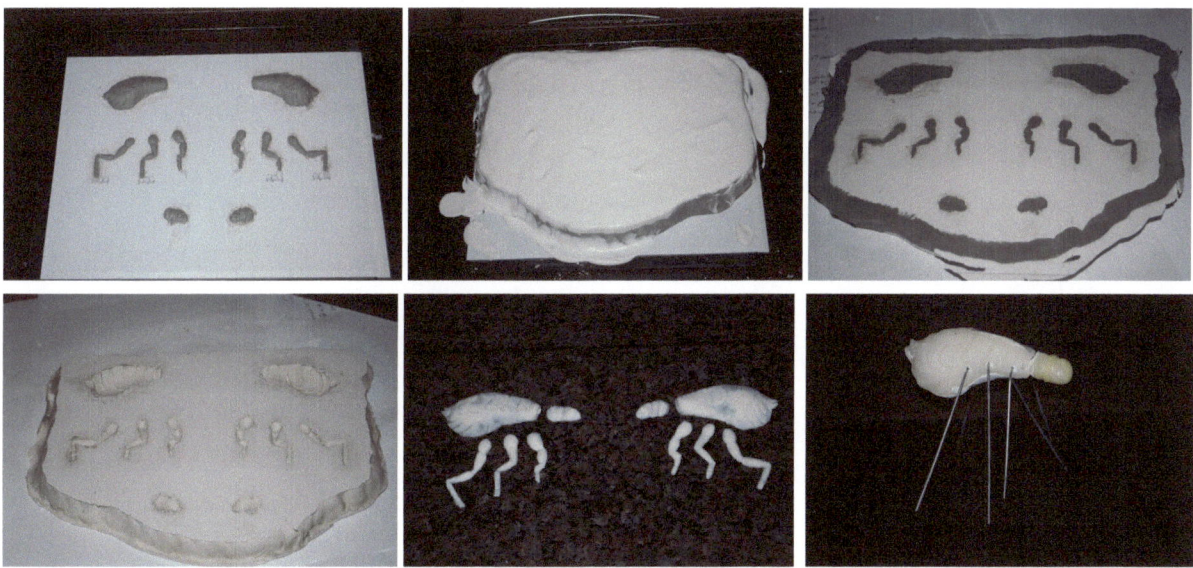

From this point it was a case of attaching all the limbs and applying the 'muscles' in the form of latex and wool build-ups.

The prototype flea looked very 'flea-like', but it looked *too* flea-like. Neil wanted the audience to empathize with the characters, and that would be hard to do if the fleas grossed them out.

The two images below show 'proto-flea' in all his glory (minus his boots). Though considered too creepy, he would be used extensively in the early sessions during which the crew would experiment with the camera rig.

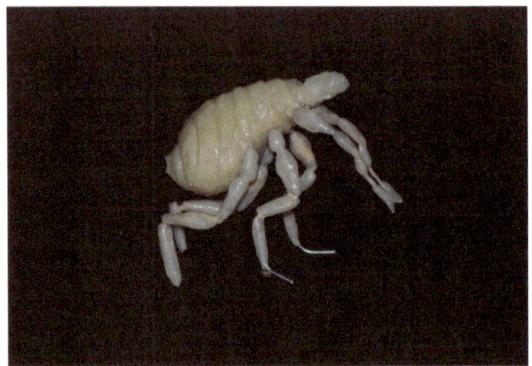 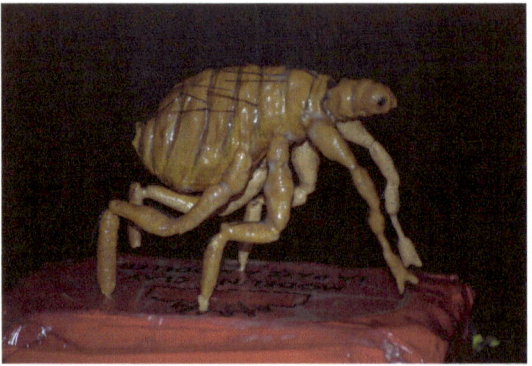

Undaunted, Neil redesigned the look of the fleas, making them more appealing, and with the help of Keenan, George, Jon and Roberta, assembled a batch of flea bodies ready to be accessorized.

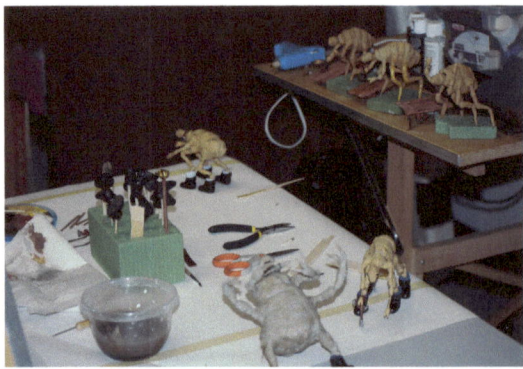 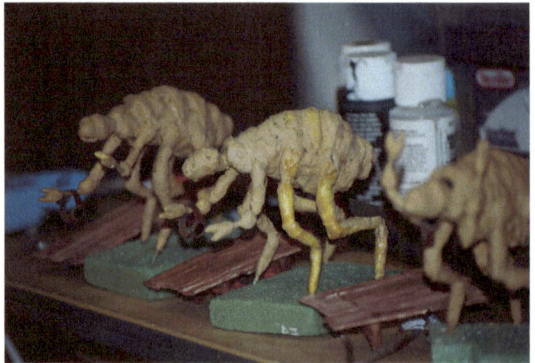

In the above photos, you can see the new fleas in an early stage of their development. The sculpy limbs have all been threaded onto the wire armatures, and the main bodies were shaped using Magic Smooth, a resin-based filler that can be smoothed and molded with water. After final armature adjustments these puppets would be further textured, with hair, mustaches and eyes added and given a final paint job. Next up, Count Otto Von Louse.

The Louse began life as a rough form sculpted out of high density Styrofoam (the kind used for flower arranging) and embedded with wire armature pieces. It was then a case of a direct build up of limbs and body mass using the same latex and cotton wool technique used before. By building him up in this fashion, the medium took on an organic quality and dictated some of the shapes and swirls that pepper his torso. Tiny Sculpy eyes were set in his eye sockets and had small holes in the pupils, which is a standard technique used by animators to move the eyes with a pin during filming.

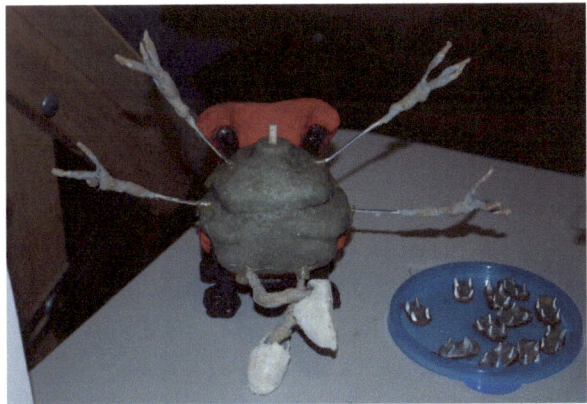 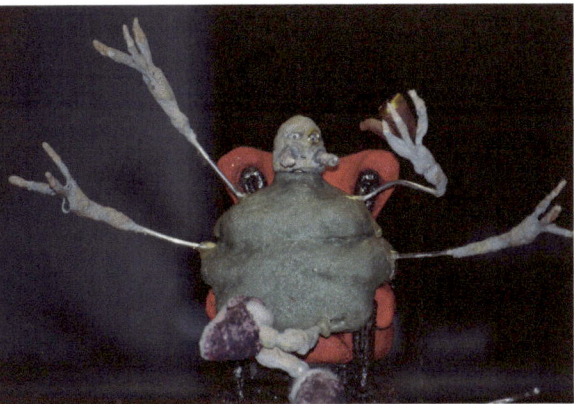

The above photos show the same technique being applied to the seated Louse, which was a separate puppet from the walking Louse. Otto needed his clothing and equipment, so tiny props were made (see next chapter) while Neil fabricated his lederhosen. First, Neil sculpted the lederhosen in clay and made a mold, then applied thin layers of latex until he had built up a sheet of mock 'leather', which could then be painted and attached to the Louse. His hat was sculpted from the Styrofoam, paintbrush bristles were used for his hat brush, and a tiny brass ring served as his monocle. A three-stage paint job, and he was ready to meet his fellow mountaineers.

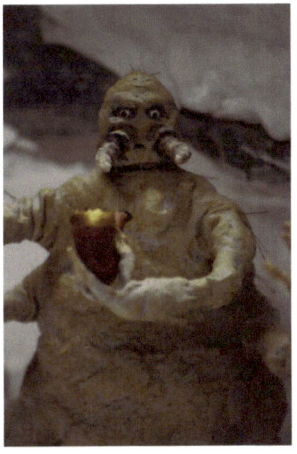 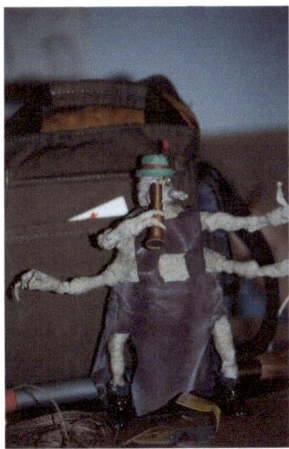 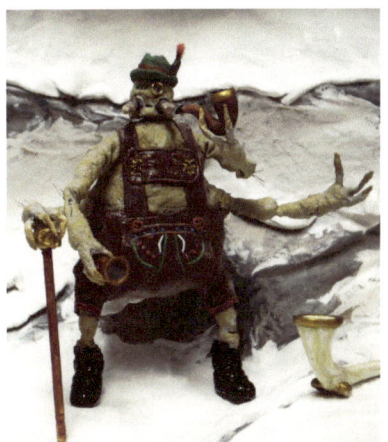

Small Stuff

The world of Small Sacrifices not only needed its geography and inhabitants, but also the various items and paraphernalia that would help to enrich each and every scene. Often overlooked by audiences, props usually have more work put into them than anything else on set, as they have to fit the story and still look believable.

Some props were 'ready-mades', items that Neil hunted down in hobby and toyshops and 'refurbished' for the expedition team. These included the boots that the insects wore (really boots from cheap, dollar store, soldiers) and various items being carried on the backpacks (mostly kit-bashed from existing military model kits).

In the following images, you can clearly see some of the 'ready-mades' in place.

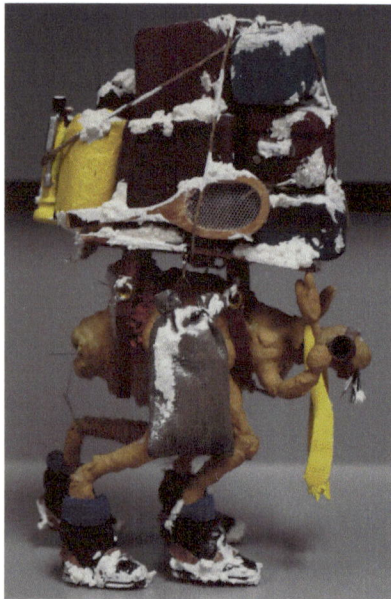 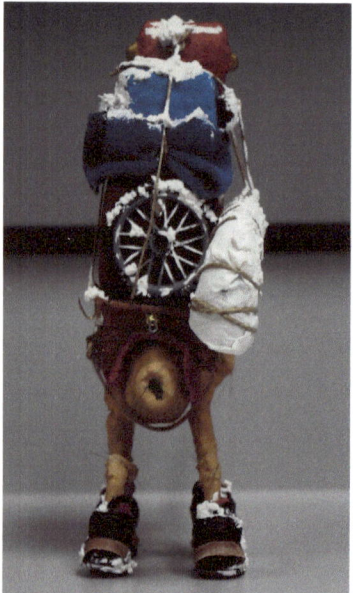 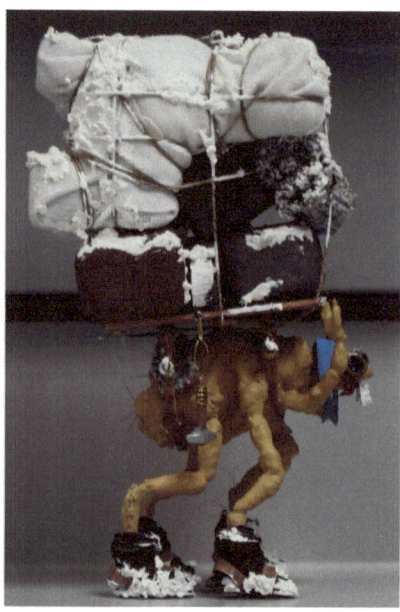

In other cases, many of the props and clothing items had to be made from scratch. For example, it would be easy to overlook the wooden platforms that the fleas are using to carry the luggage, but these are intricate little props built by Phil out of wood and accessorized with latex 'leather' straps and brass hooks by Neil. The strap buckles were fashioned from sculpy and painted.

The rolled up blankets that the fleas are carrying are scraps of sock and tee shirt material (as are their actual socks), and the cases are all carved from high-density foam and painted with an acrylic and latex mix. The fleas' scarves were actually pieces of wire sandwiched between thin strips of cotton material and painted with acrylic and latex which left them flexible enough to be animated but firm enough to retain their shape.

The goggles are sculpy lenses glued onto latex straps, and around 30 individual crampons were made by Jon for scenes when the insects lifted their boots, revealing a space where spikes should be.

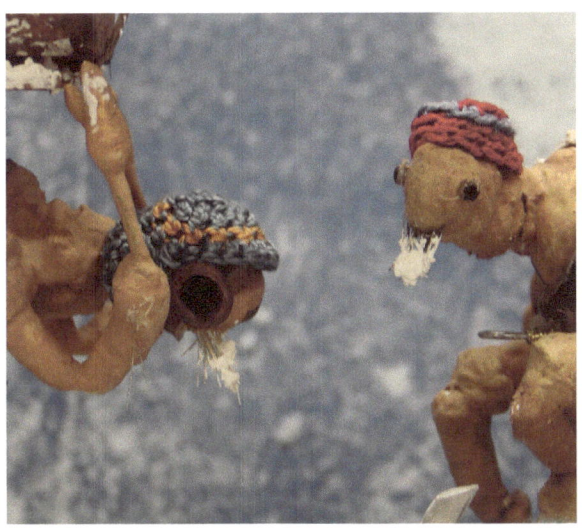 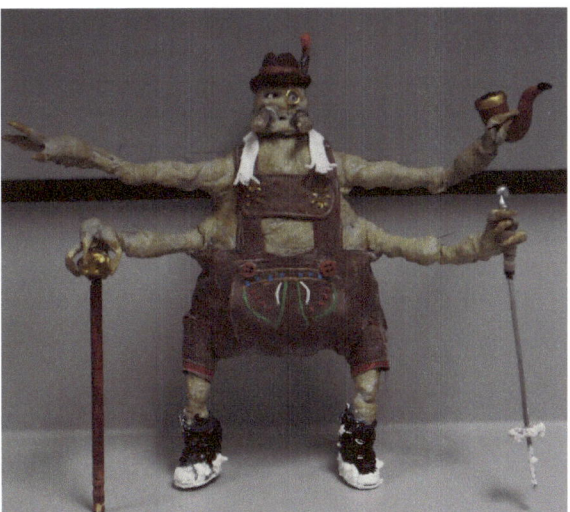

It was decided early on that an identifier was needed to separate the fleas from one another, and different colored scarves were one solution. Another was to get Roberta, the film's resident knitter, to actually crochet some tiny hats for the two 'scout' fleas. This she did with great aplomb, thus earning the unique film credit 'Flea Milliner'.

Count Otto Von Louse needed to be attired with clothes and items that really accentuated his character. To this end, not only was he outfitted in some well-worn lederhosen and an Alpine trilby, but he also had a tiny brass monocle fitted, an aviator's scarf (suggesting past exploits), an elaborate pipe and two walking sticks. One stick was a ski pole, which seems out of place; part of an incomplete set, and hints at past disasters, and the other is a walking cane complete with a beautifully sculpted headpiece by Phil. This headpiece is in the shape of a gold insect head, perhaps suggesting the grip Otto has over his insect team. Keenan used all of these props to their utmost when animating the louse, making them an extension of Otto's body and helping to highlight the more subtle actions in some shots.

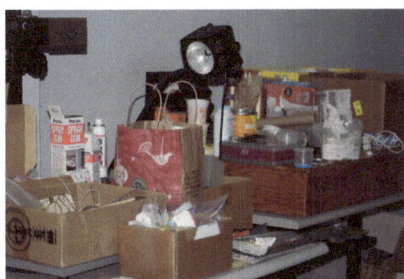 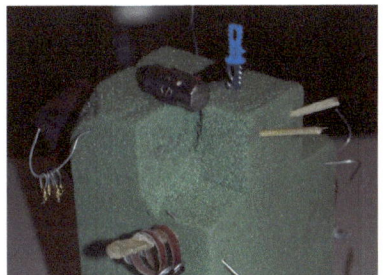 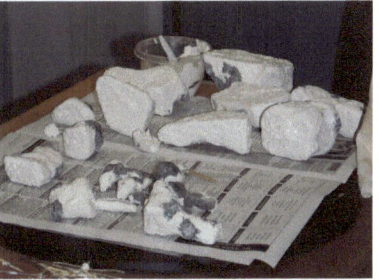

Above are images showing our 'go to' area for prop-making materials, hooks, goggles and ready-mades waiting for action, and a collection of Styrofoam rocks in the process of being painted, ready for placement on the set and for their big avalanche scene.

Some of the more elaborate props would require careful planning and construction, and these included the camera, the gramophone and the flag.

As George is an excellent model-maker and meticulous in his detailing, he stepped up to create the majority of these items. Firstly, Neil sent him a rough plan of the camera, and George responded with computer simulations of the prop, and finally the prop itself. The mandate for this item was that it was to look old-fashioned, yet have the mechanisms of a modern Polaroid camera. George was able to construct a tiny model that not only opened up with a concertina-style lens and developing tray, but also with a working flash bulb!

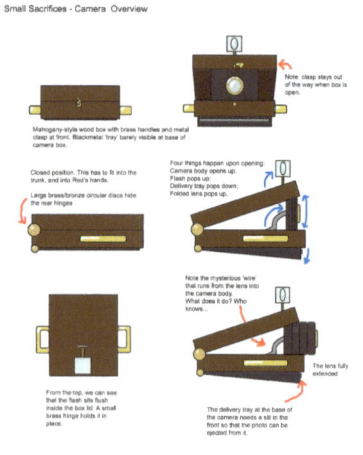
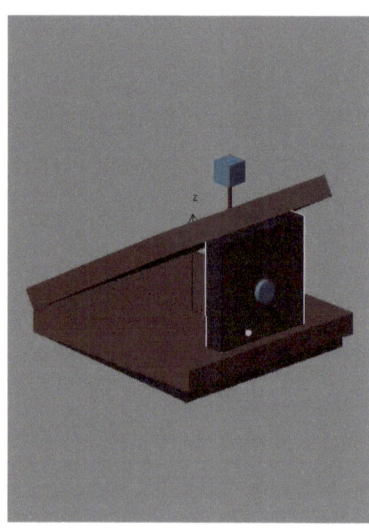
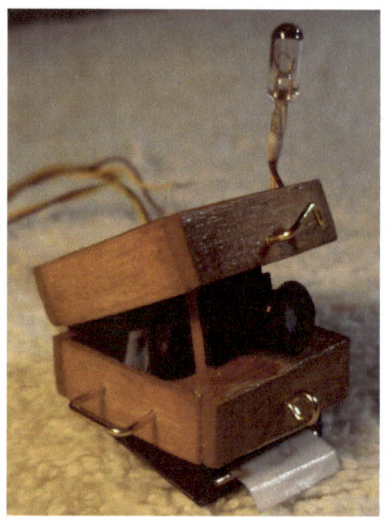

While George had a hand in the flagpole and box building, the flag itself was made by Roberta by gluing fabric to aluminum foil and painting on a design that was initially created by Phil and then refined by Neil. The box was hinged and had a tiny clasp, and the flagpole was made up of five individual lengths connected by tiny hinges that allowed the Louse to unfold it before planting it.

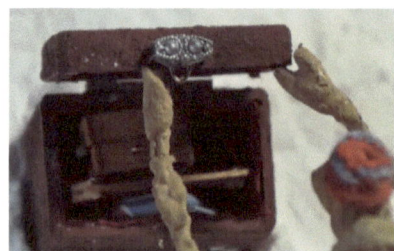
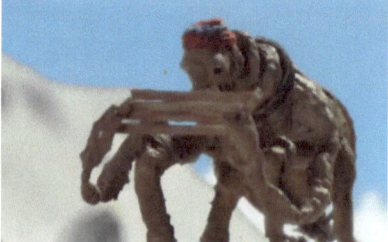
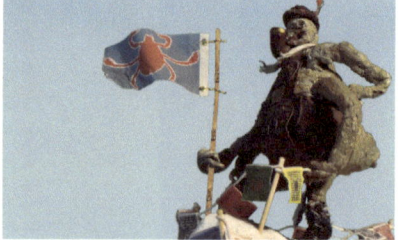

As with all the props, these items looked functional and believable, and were brought to life through interaction with the insects and some terrific animation from Keenan and Roberta.

The Cabin

Following the initial designs, George built a cardboard version of the cabin so that we could test it with regard to scale and lighting options against the mountain set. Note the cutout bug stand-ins. He then went ahead and built the final wooden cabin with wild walls, which meant any configuration of structure could be assembled for ease of camera and light placement.

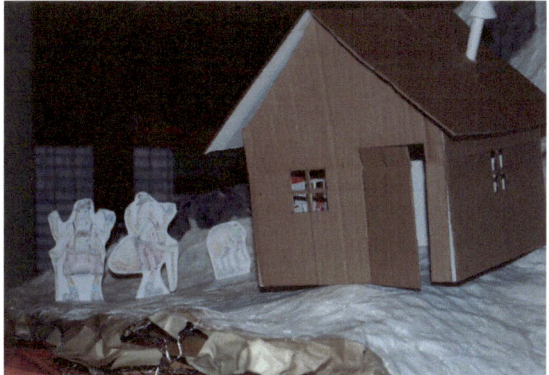 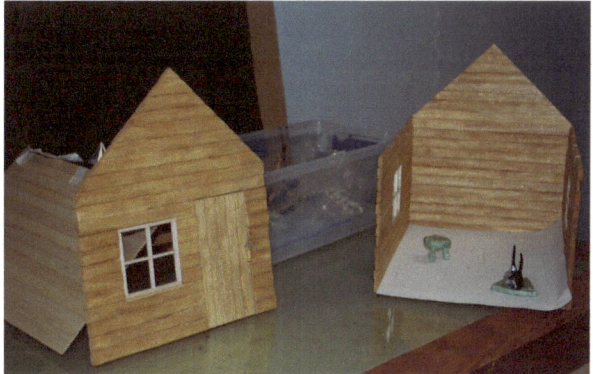

George not only made the cabin with wild walls, but he also provided a removable roof, replacement shingles (should there be any shots where the snow has melted around the chimney) and a hinged front door with external latch and internal locking bar.

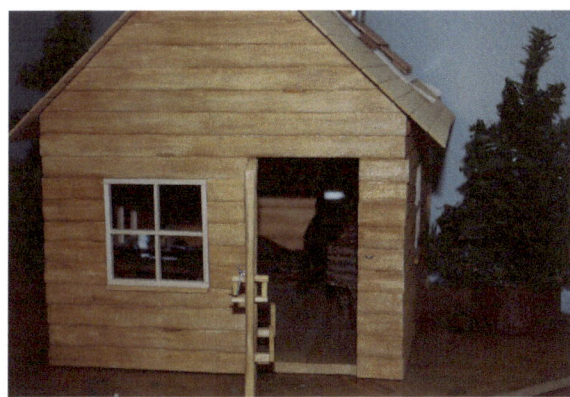 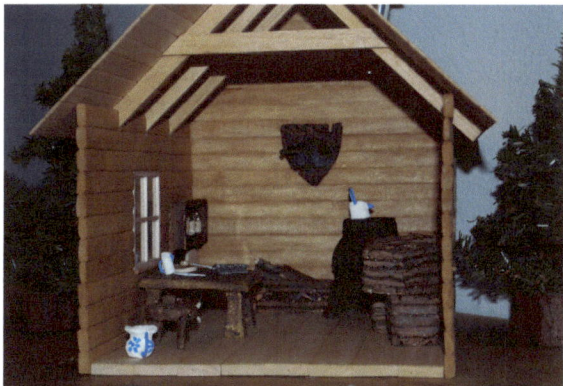

The internal rafters of the roof gave the whole structure much more stability, and easily supported a secondary roof piece that Neil fabricated which was comprised of card, latex, cotton wool and powder and used to simulate the layers of snow.

The furniture and other items for the interior of the cabin were first sculpted from high-density foam and then coated with a latex and paint solution before their final detailing and weathering was applied. In some cases, ready-found objects were used, such as some local twigs that worked well for stove logs, and a toy beetle that was kit-bashed into a mounted 'trophy'.

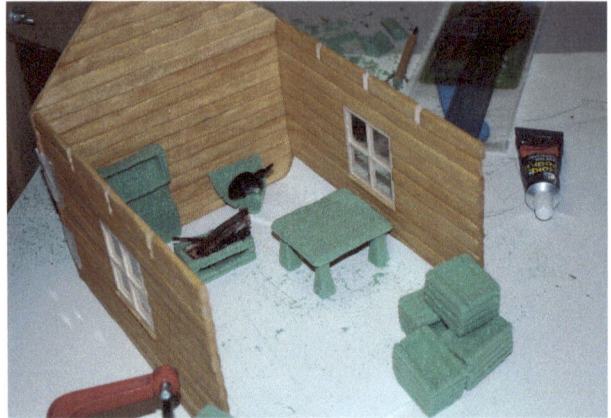 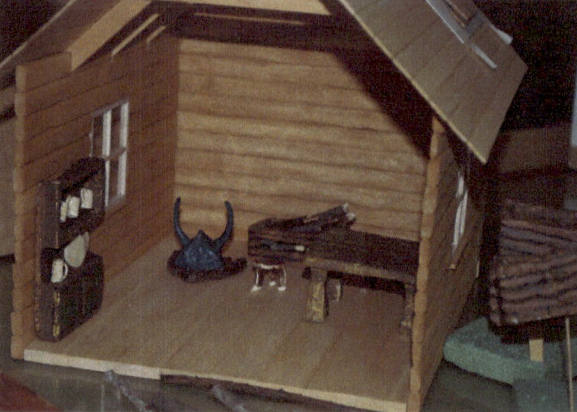

It was then a case of populating the cabin with enough items to make it look well used and practical.

In the first photograph, you will see the table and stool and a small dresser complete with cups and plates. These items were actually sculpted in clay, glazed and fired by Jon. Jon also included tiny items of cutlery and a chamber pot (contents unknown). A collection of motley packing crates filled another corner by the door and Phil's stove rested in the adjoining corner with a small coffee pot (also by Jon) on its hotplate. At this point, the interior chimney had not been inserted.

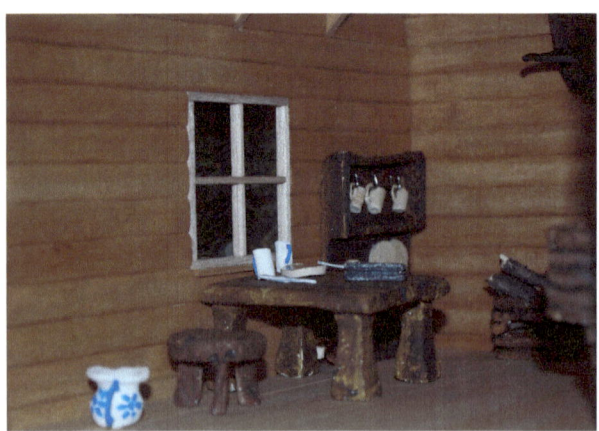 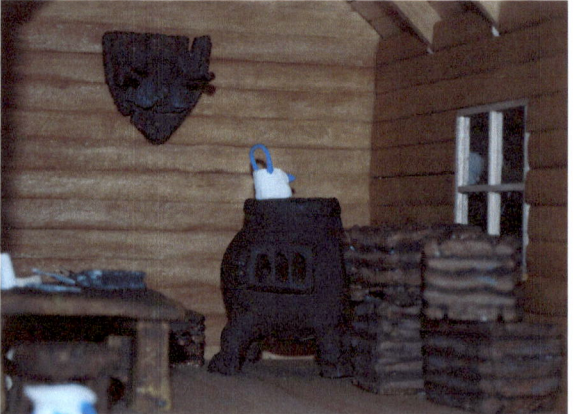

It was now ready for final touches, including interior weathering and other items of furniture.

One of the final touches to be placed in the cabin was a tiny dartboard, complete with chalkboard and three miniscule darts. Once the cabin was populated and lit, it provided exactly the right setting for one of the key scenes in the film, when the Louse displays his true colors at the expense of his freezing team.

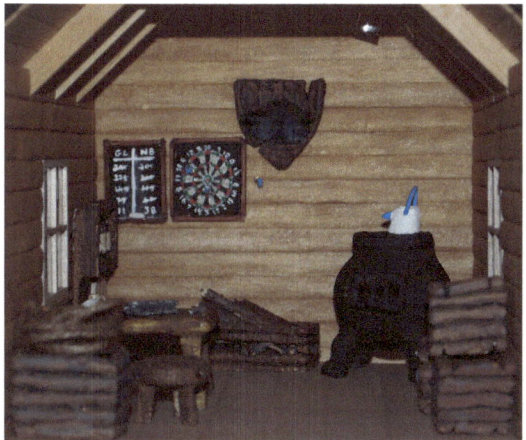 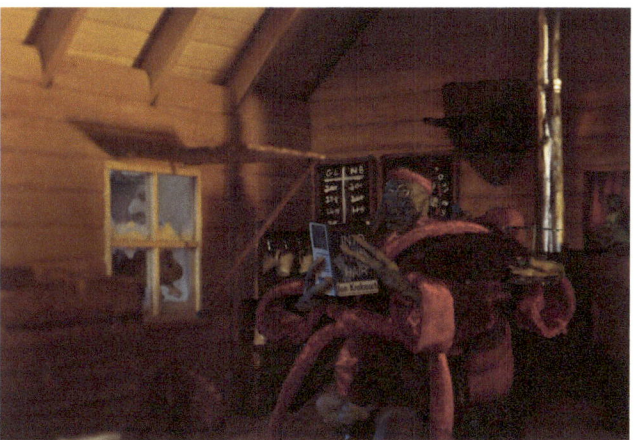

If you look closely, behind the stovepipe you will notice a small poster on the cabin wall. This is one of two posters that Neil requested from Phil. Neil wanted the sense that other lonely travelers had used this cabin and left their mark, and a couple of girly pin-ups seemed to fit the bill. Neil and Phil researched cheesecake illustrations from the 30's, 40's and 50's, and used classic poses by Marilyn Monroe and Bettie Page as inspiration for the two extraordinary paintings Phil delivered, reprinted in all their glory here.

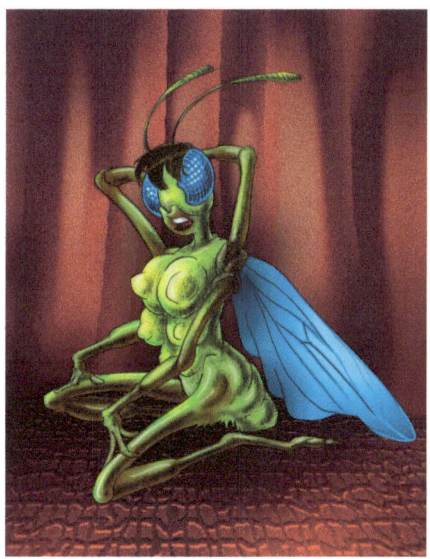 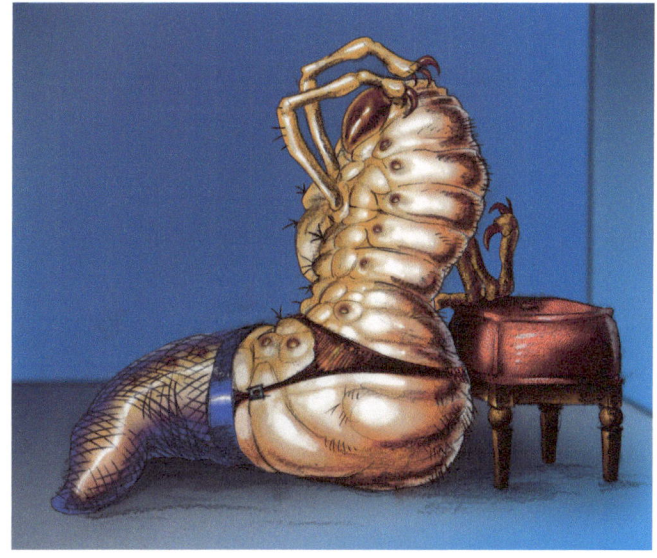

Filming the Climb

Once the majority of the physical props, sets and puppets were in place, principle photography could begin. The shoot would take pace over a 16-month period in a specially designed 'cage', located in the film studio belonging to the creative arts division of De Anza. The cage was a self-contained unit, with storage and overhead lighting rigs, and would serve as a shooting stage and storage area. Neil's storyboards and Phil's concept art adorned the back wall, and the flea puppets awaited their cues.

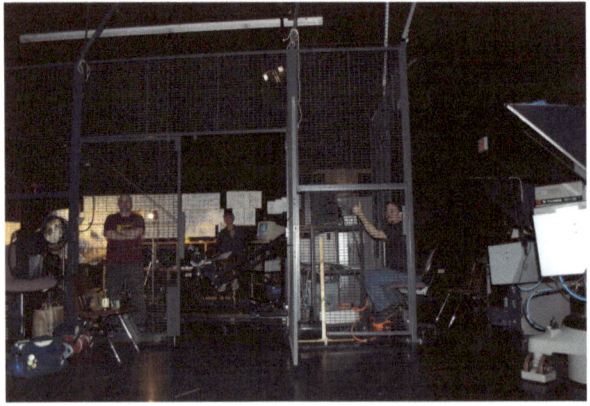 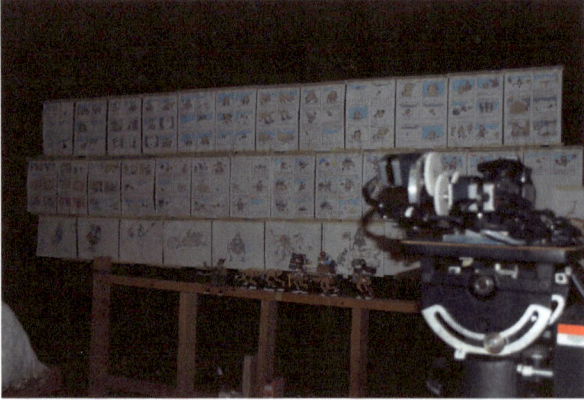

Early on in the pre-production phase, it was decided to shoot the film as single frame jpeg images using a digital camera. This meant that we could shoot at 4K resolution (the same as most modern digital blockbusters) and would give us more freedom in the post-production stages to crop and digitally composite the shots while still maintaining a high definition image. The camera that was used was a Nikon D-90 with a fixed 55-200mm Tamron lens. This lens, combined with the shooting range, would provide the short depth of field required for the look of the film. The camera and its motion-control rig was built on fixed dolly tracks by Tim Taylor, who is one of the world's leading motion-control filmmakers, and who has worked on such productions as *Coraline* and *James and the Giant Peach*.

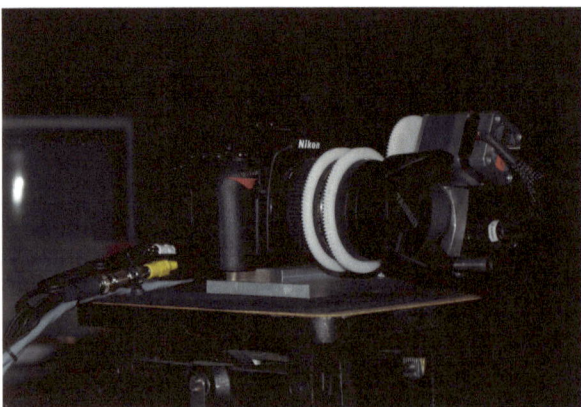 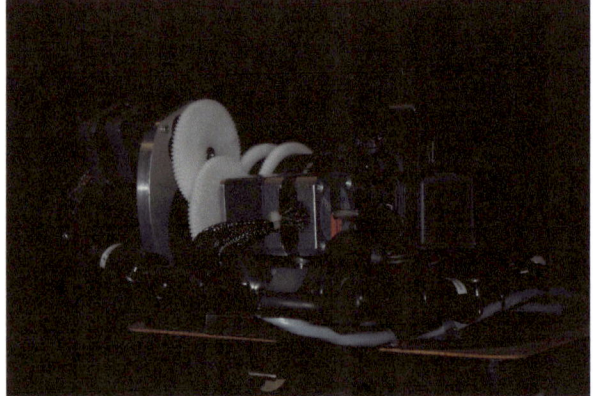

While the camera was controlled by a computer running the Kuper Motion Control program, a separate camera was also set up to capture the animation in progress and which fed the frames into a separate laptop where they were captured using MonkeyJam for immediate playback. The Nikon was also feeding the camera images into another monitor via a traditional animator's 'lunchbox', which meant multiple angles were available for reference during animation. Note: the snow on the cabin below is temporary!

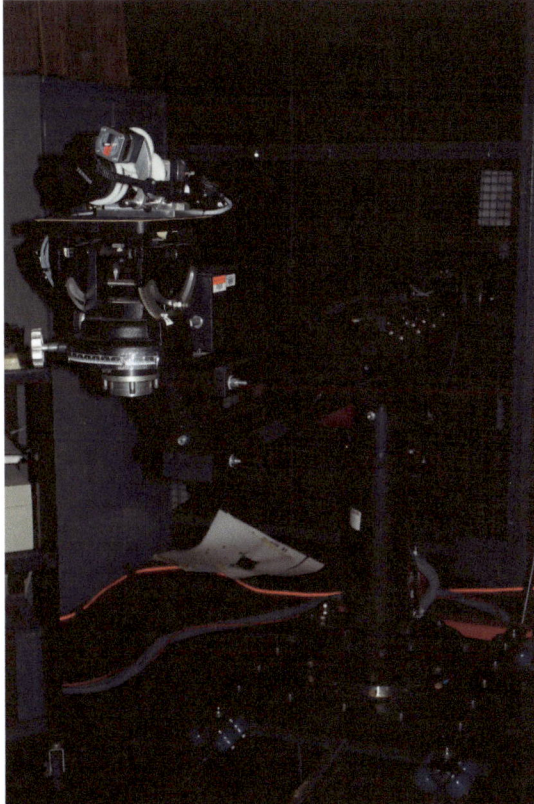 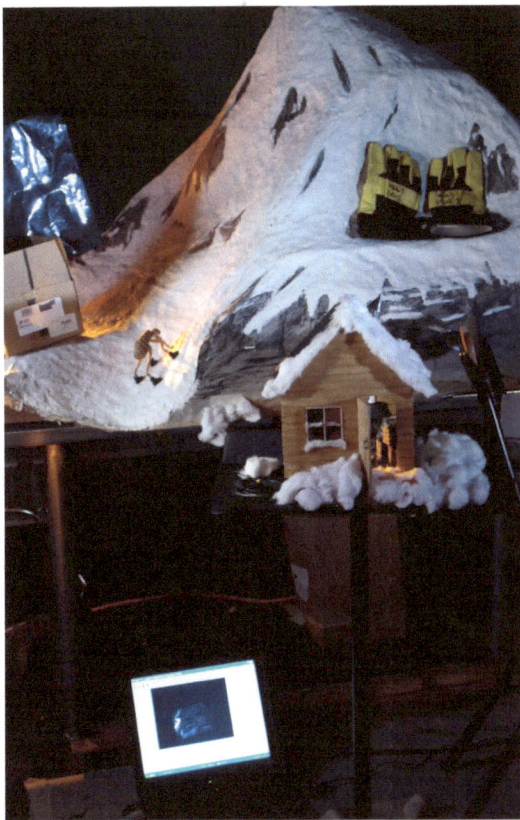

All of the raw frames were captured onto 8GB memory cards, which were regularly taken home by Neil and Keenan and backed up in three separate locations. Part of the challenge of filming with the Kuper system was learning the commands and techniques to make the camera move incrementally one frame at a time for 12 frames a second; including ease in and ease out effects and some elaborate multiple moves. For this reason, Neil, Keenan, Roberta, Jon and a newer crew member, Chris Jackson, made sure that there would always be someone on set who knew their way around the controls and, more importantly, knew how to avoid crunching the delicate gears.

The production used a variety of lights, from tiny sprinklers to overhead 1 and 2K lamps. Various gels and diffusers were used to capture different times of the day, and in most cases the shots would be slightly over lit, as it was always the intention in post-production to crush the saturation of the colors down to create an older feel to the final image.

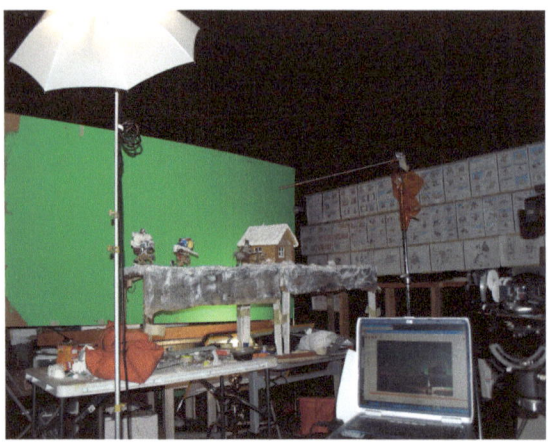 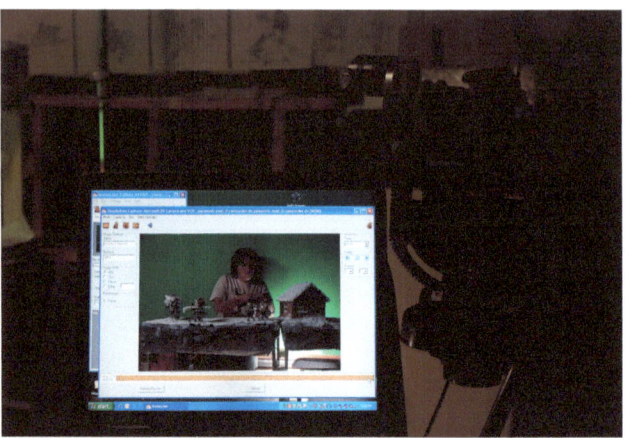

The above images show a typical set up, in this case scene 3 shot 2, which shows the approach to the cabin. Through storyboarding and discussion the crew had already established what elements would be needed for the shot, and in this case, just the puppets, the cabin and a surface for them to walk on. The rest of the mountain would be added in post-production using either a CG model or shots of the practical model. Note the umbrella reflector for the lamp, giving the shot a soft light and thus avoiding hard shadows. The view on the laptop monitor shows Keenan setting up one frame of action.

Below is a shot from the same scene that depicts 'Red', one of the flea scouts, in mid-jump. This image was taken directly from the monitor screen, and exemplifies what Keenan, Roberta and Neil would see as they were animating. Note the rig support for Red. This rigging was actually a tiny articulated clamp system usually used for fine detail model making or jewelry making. These rigs turned out to be perfect for positioning the puppets when they were unable to be locked down onto the set. A small clamp at one end could be unceremoniously inserted into the fleas' rear-ends or used to clamp their hind legs, and were prominent enough to make painting out easy. The second photo shows Neil, Jon and Keenan adjusting the rigging for the shot – Roberta is monitoring the move off set.

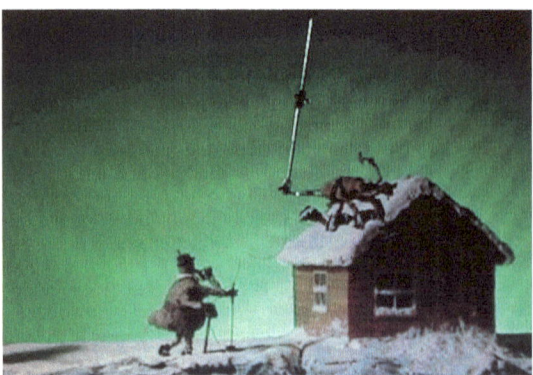 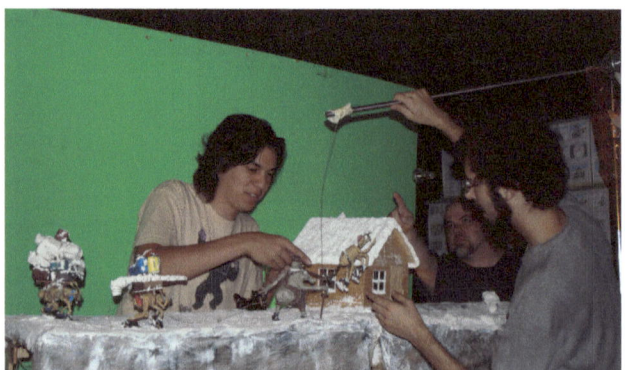

In some cases the production crew had to get inventive with the set placement. For one or two shots, extreme angles were required, and luckily the 'table-top' sets were light enough that they could be manipulated into any position using C-stands and gobo arms.

In the images below, two of the small sets have been positioned and clamped on their sides for an intricate shot that would show the POV (point of view) of one of the fleas as he looks over the edge to see his colleague laying dead on an outcropping below. The motion control camera rig was positioned so that the lens would boom up and then focus on the dead flea below. The first image shows the set up from a side angle, and the second demonstrates how the shot would eventually look on the raw footage. In post-production, the green screen would be removed and replaced by a matte painting from Phil before color correction was applied.

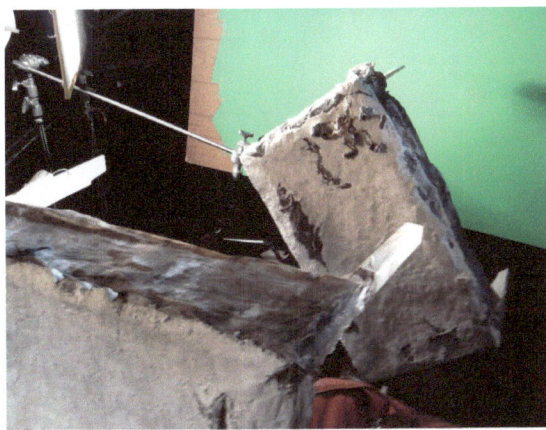 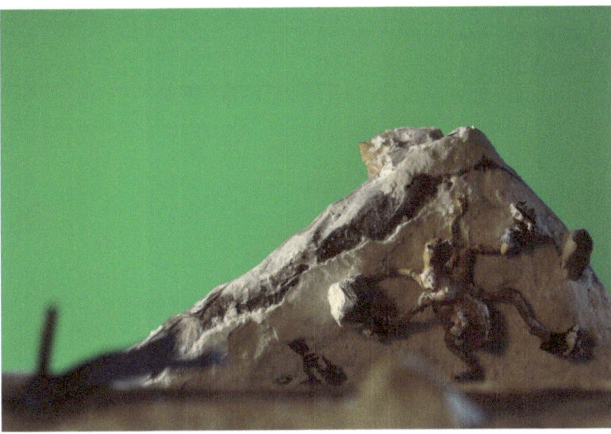

In other instances, the same sets could be set up to replicate specific angled slopes and backgrounds. Below, Roberta applies the finishing touches including some detailed snow wrangling to a shot near the end of the film, and next to that is the finished shot as it appears in the film (minus falling snow).

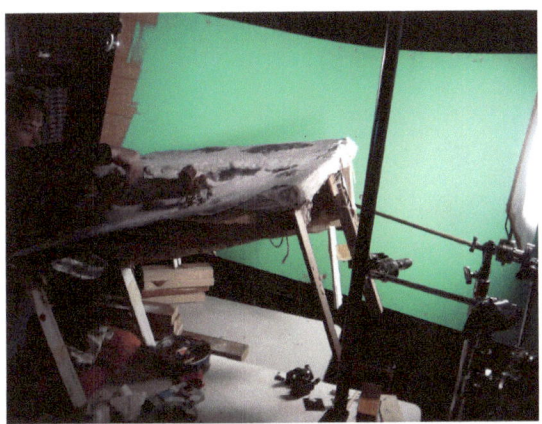 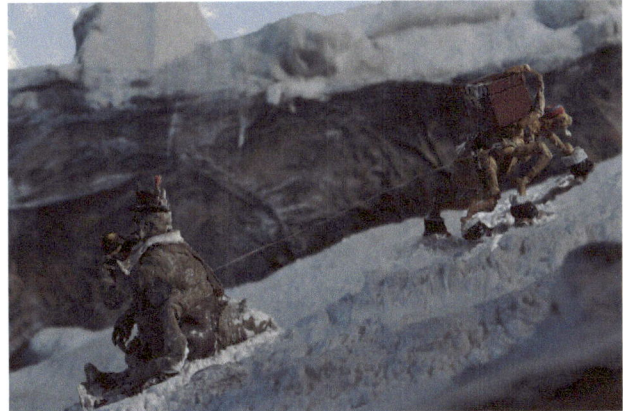

Smoke and Mirrors

With the bulk of the footage safely in the digital 'can', the production team could now focus on the post-production requirements, namely the compositing and rendering of the shots using After Effects, Photoshop, Premiere and Maya.

Seeing as seven eighths of the film took place during snowfall, it was established early on that a system would be needed to created different forms of snowfall as well as be easily used by the compositors. To this end, Keenan designed a snowfall simulator using Maya software that would incorporate multi-plane surfaces and focal distances. He then scanned clumps of baking powder and imported the individual random shapes into his program. The result was a very realistic snowfall effect that could be simply applied to the composited footage in different layers and scales, and according to wind speed and direction.

Keenan's original scans of baking powder clusters.   A still frame from a snowfall sequence that will be added to the final shots.

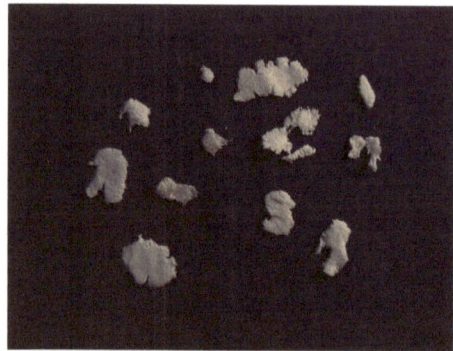

The crew also organized a practical effects session, which was recorded on HD video for later insertion into the film. This was an opportunity to create realistic atmospheric effects including fog and mist, powder impacts and puffs and rock-falls for the avalanche scene. Below, Keenan oversees the lighting of a fog bank, while off-camera, Roberta, Bill Dwan (who would later head the CG team) and Neil operate smoke machines and fans in order to create the exact type of swirls needed for the shot. By cooling down the fog, they were able to make it linger menacingly in the trench.

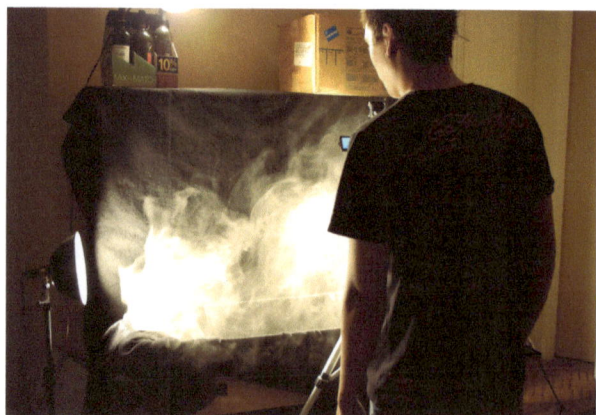
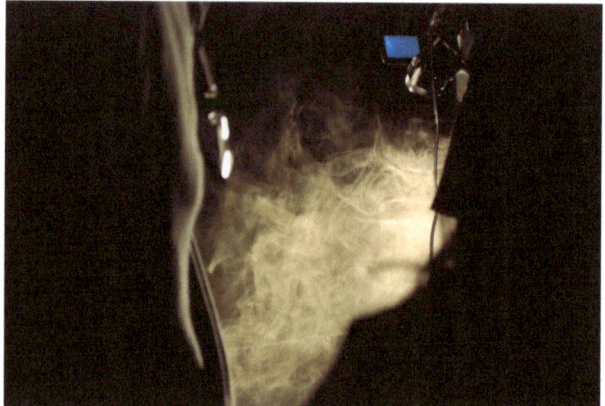

During the compositing stage of the film, Neil recruited several more talented friends to join the crew, including Rob Pendleton, Alix Herrmann and Chris Jackson, as well as himself, Jon, Keenan and Roberta. Compositing takes on many different forms; some shots are straightforward and require only snowfall to be added, others might need green screen removal and background plates inserted, and others might be much more complex, as the following sequence by Keenan demonstrates.

The shot in scene 2 of the first flea dying by falling into a chasm involves a camera move as well as a multitude of elements.

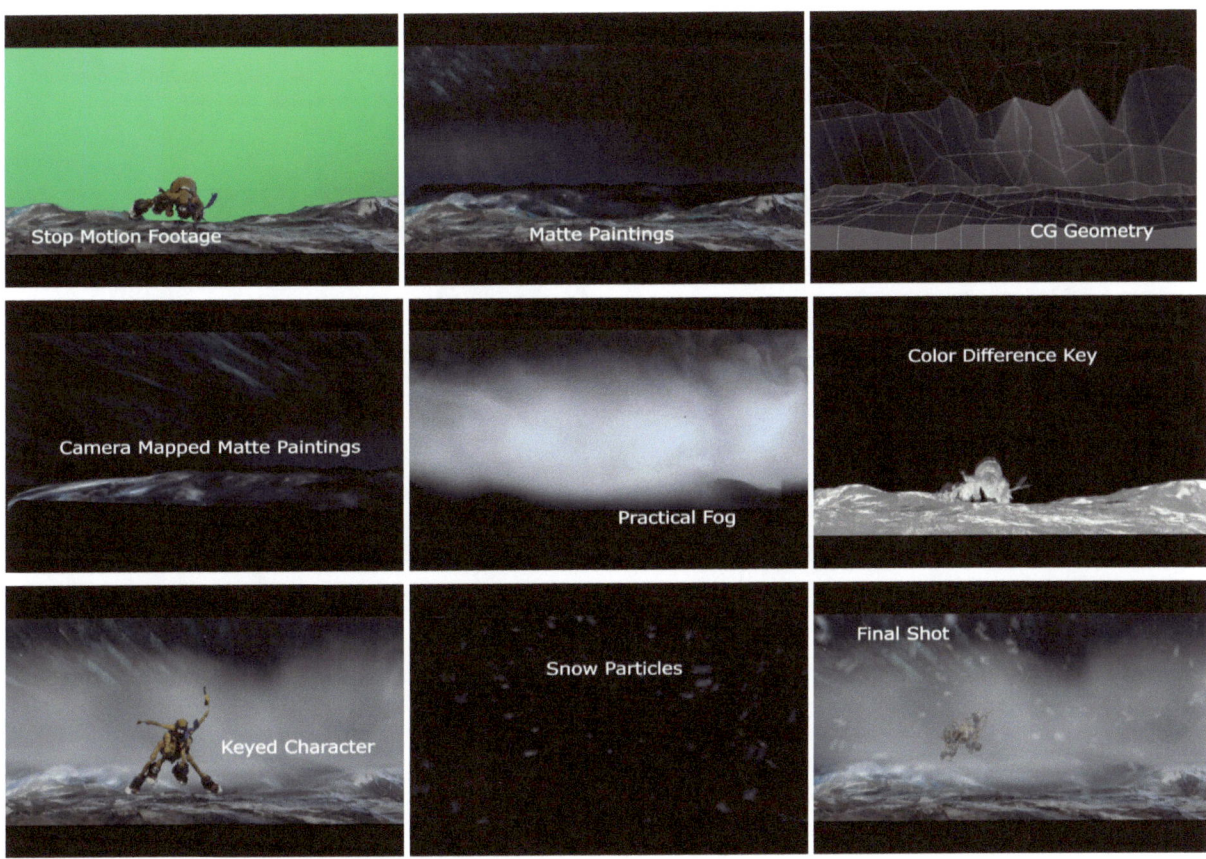

There are actually several more stages not included in the above collection, but just from these examples you will begin to understand the level of complexity of some of these shots.

If nothing else, working on *Small Sacrifices* has offered the entire crew the opportunity to not only push their own skills to the limit, but to also develop new skills, techniques and work-arounds in order to achieve the final goals

Computer Bugs

Early on in the pre-production stages it had been established that some element of computer-generated animation would need to be employed in order to achieve some particular shots. As the production was underway, the CG shots increased as it became apparent that this tool would be perfect for establishing shots and creating sweeping camera moves that were impossible to achieve with the camera rig. To this end, Bill Dwan was brought on to head a digital team due to his extensive skills as a 3D animator, modeler and rigger, and he began to churn out a plethora of animated shots that would blend seamlessly into the puppet footage, aided by George and some additional modelers, Eileen Laitinen and Naomi Meyers, who sculpted luggage and backpacks..

Bill began by fleshing out the bugs. He based his initial models on the concept art and puppet footage available to him, and slowly the team began to take shape. As the bugs would never be seen in close up, Bill had some flexibility with the level of texturing required.

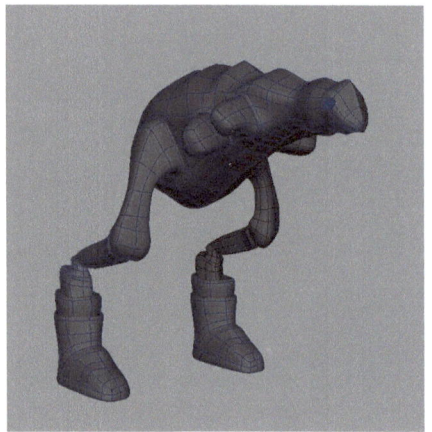
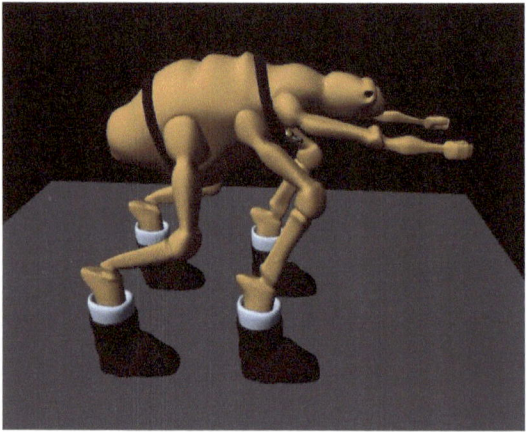

During this evolutionary process, Neil and Keenan supplied Bill with a series of diagrams indicating the movement of the fleas.

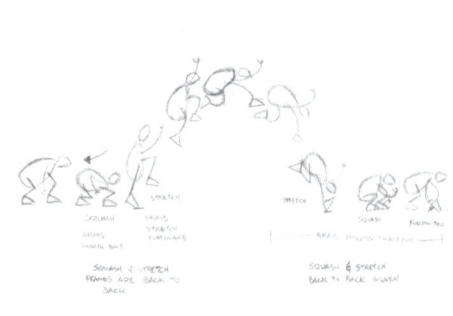
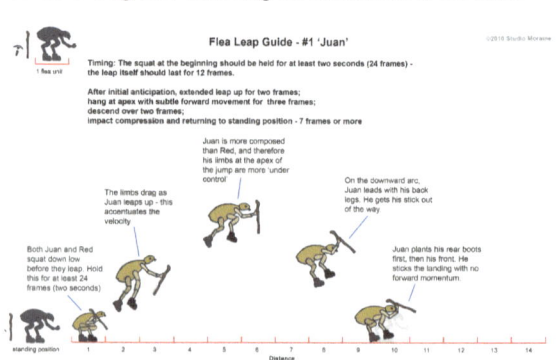

As the CG models developed, Bill started to tackle the Louse and also provided examples of walk cycles. It became important to realize how distinct each of the bugs were when it came to movement, as they all had their own individual personalities and characteristics. The two scouts had markedly different jump patterns due to their age and experience, the 'pack-fleas' had different walking stances based on their loads, and the louse developed a waddling gait with his two sticks becoming extensions of his forelimbs.

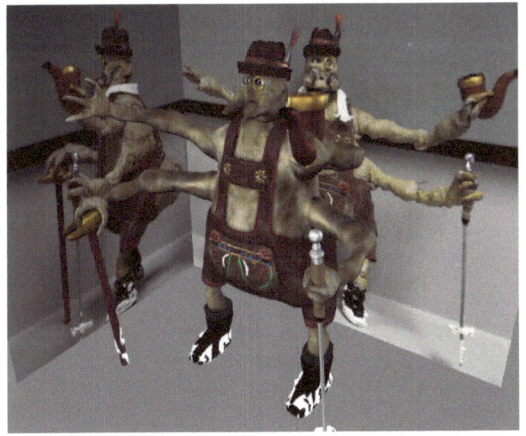 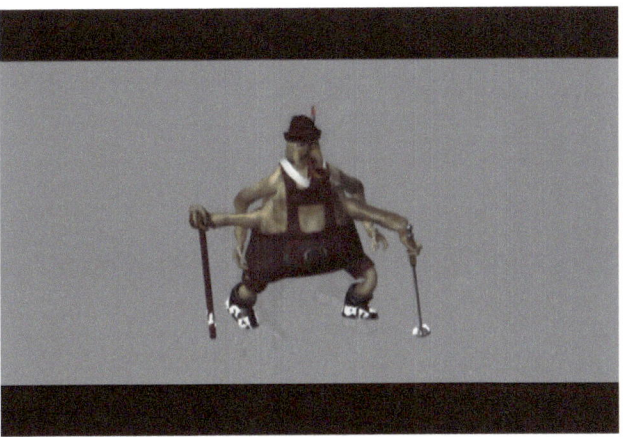

At the same time, George was taking Bill's models into a program called Carrara, and experimenting with eye blinks and footprints. Though successful, it was deemed unnecessary for the eyes to blink, as their distance was too great. The footprints, however, were a good idea, and Bill later used this scheme in his rendered shots.

The images below show displaced snow around the flea's boots, and the full team (minus their completed backpacks).

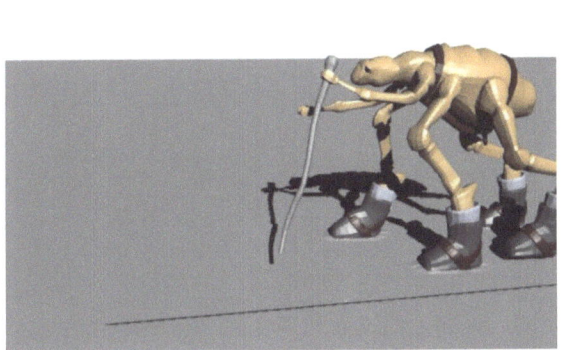 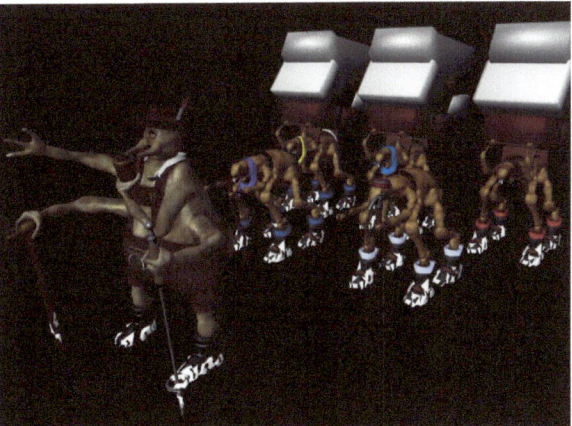

With the team in place, it was now time to turn our attention to the mountain.

Using concept art from Neil, Phil and Keenan, Bill was able to create the entire mountain in Maya, which could be tweaked and adapted to suit the various locations needed for specific scenes. Neil could then use this basic version of the mountain, plus Bill's bug models, and create simple animatic of the missing shots so that the timing and choreography could be established before Bill began the real animation.

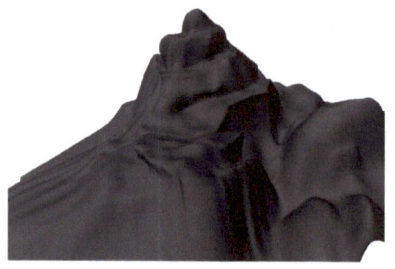 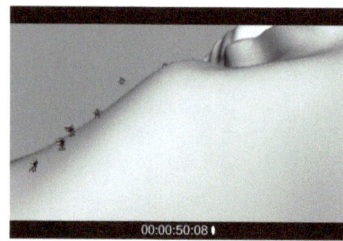 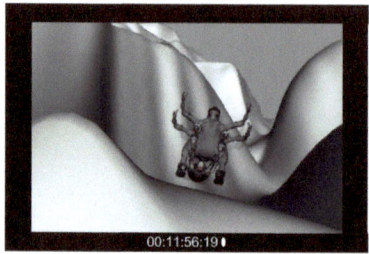

In many cases Neil was able to use the simple animatics and coordinate with Bill in designing more dynamic geography and angles. A prime example is the 'ice ring'. The above middle and right frames show the initial introduction to the climbing fleas, and the final shot as the louse rides a flea down the mountain in triumph. Neil wanted to establish a geographical feature that would bookend the film and help the audience identify the amount of terrain covered. To this end, he came up with the concept of an ice ring or arch that the bugs would traverse through at the beginning of the film, and that would frame the louse in a freeze-frame shot at the film's conclusion. Bill delivered the structure and elaborated upon the rest of the terrain, making everything seem even more perilous.

Bill's new opening shot with ice arch and bridge   Bill's new closing shot

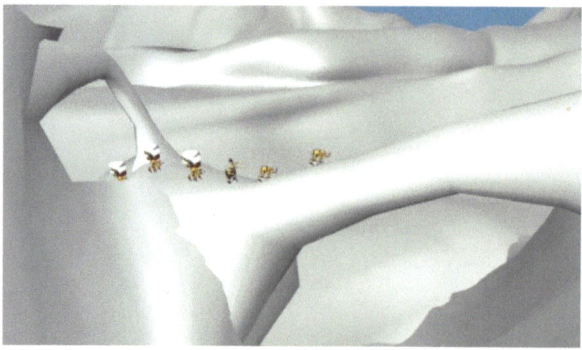 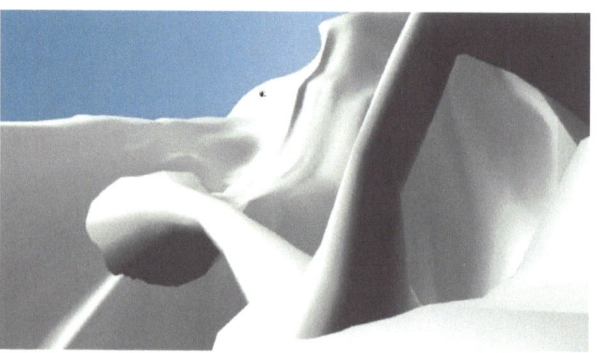

With the terrain in place it was now necessary to texture and light the geography to match the physical set. Bill used numerous set photographs and texture programs to simulate the snow effect that had been achieved during the filming process, and many discussions took place regarding the placement of the sun and how each CG shot would flow into the puppet shots. This is a monumental workload and, at time of printing, the experimentation was still in progress. However, on the following page, you can see some examples of the texturing and lighting in progress.

Below is the opening scene with added snow texturing and lighting effects. Note that the tether ropes are missing, as is the snow. Bill managed to make a convincing tether effect using hair simulators built into Maya, and these ropes flow and react with each leap from the fleas. Next to this shot is another from later in the film, showing the scale of the team's challenge.

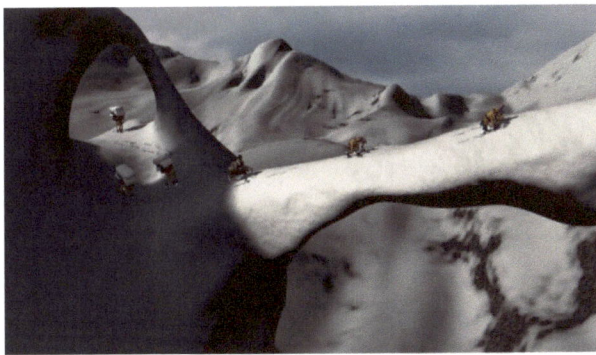 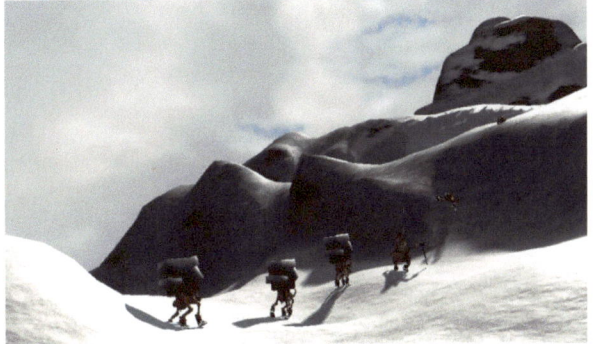

For the final scene in which we watch the louse sledding down the mountain on the corpse of his last flea scout, Neil, Bill and Keenan decided on a mixture of puppet and CG shots to illustrate the macabre yet exhilarating event. For the final shot, Bill got the geography looking just right, and tested the framing with his CG louse. Then Keenan and Roberta filmed a series of images of the puppet louse riding the puppet flea on a turntable, so that any of the images could be later inserted into the CG environment. Below is an early test of this, you can see the green outline of the green screen around the louse, but this will be refined and corrected in the final version.

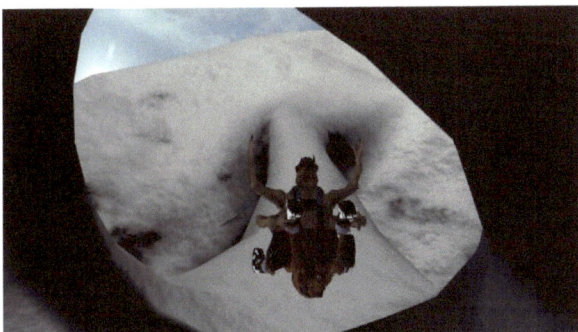 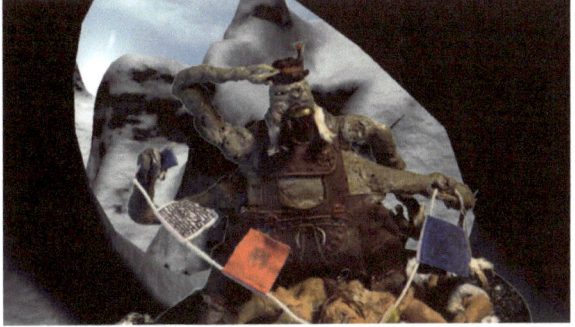

As well as texturing the terrain, and animating the bugs, Bill also added various little touches that would further enhance the images. He used a wind simulation in the scarves of the bugs to add more movement to their forms and, following George's initial experiments, Bill has included footprints and other scuff marks to the shots. With other elements such as the compositing of practical fog and powder puffs, and Keenan's CG snow, each shot will be densely layered and atmospheric.

Soundscapes

Despite the amount of pre-production, production and post that goes into any film, the image is only half of the 'picture'. A film is nothing without a compelling soundtrack, and Neil was lucky enough to obtain the services of two industry professionals to provide him with the necessary audio richness for *Small Sacrifices*.

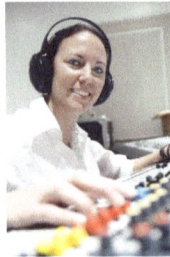

Karen Collins teaches sound design and conducts research into interactive sound at the University of Waterloo. She is currently working on an Android sound project for Google, and has just finished writing her second book about video game sound.

Karen is in the process of developing a layered audio track that not only reflects the harsh conditions of the ascent, but also highlights the tiny movements of the fleas and louse; from footfalls and vocalizations, to the strains of leather straps, jangling equipment and sleet peppering the insects hard carapaces. Her foley work for the film has included flinging particles (salt, grit, flax seed) at canvas for the sound of ice particles, and even recording the squeal of breaking ice during the spring thaw in Ontario.

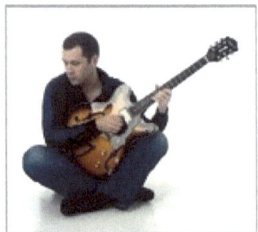

James Semple is a UK-based composer who specializes in realistic digital orchestration. Although he works predominantly via computer, James is an accomplished musician and plays guitar, piano, bass and saxophone. He has composed scores for several multi-media feature films and shorts and has released epic soundtracks based on the Cthulhu mythos created by HP Lovecraft.

For *Small Sacrifices*, James is exploring many different musical avenues in order to fully convey the majesty of the mountain, and the personality of the insects. Through video meetings with Neil, it was concluded that the film needed an epic, adventurous feel to it, and James suggested basing the score on the work of Bernard Herrmann and Max Steiner. It was also noted that, because of the Louse's European heritage, a polka would best define him (being out of place on the mountainside). Other evocative instruments such as finger cymbals and pipes would add to the tapestry of sound being woven by James and Karen.

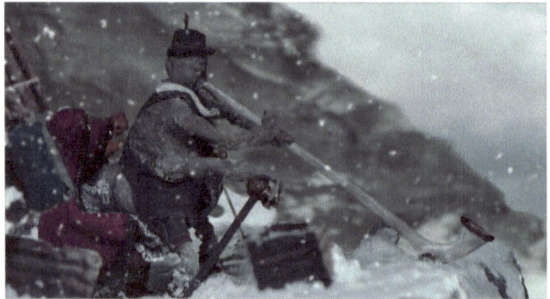

Promotion

The book you are holding in your hands is part of the promotional campaign that is de rigueur for any independent filmmakers these days. Without the big studio budgets available for spreading the word, small-scale companies must use any means possible to get the word out, and thankfully the proliferation of new media resources makes this a little easier.

Very early on in the development of the film, Neil set up a Face book group for *Small Sacrifices* as well as a blog site, where he and other crew members could post their progress for others to see. This was also a great outlet for a little advance publicity to garner interest in the film, and Neil created several documents that he posted online to help set the stage for the film.

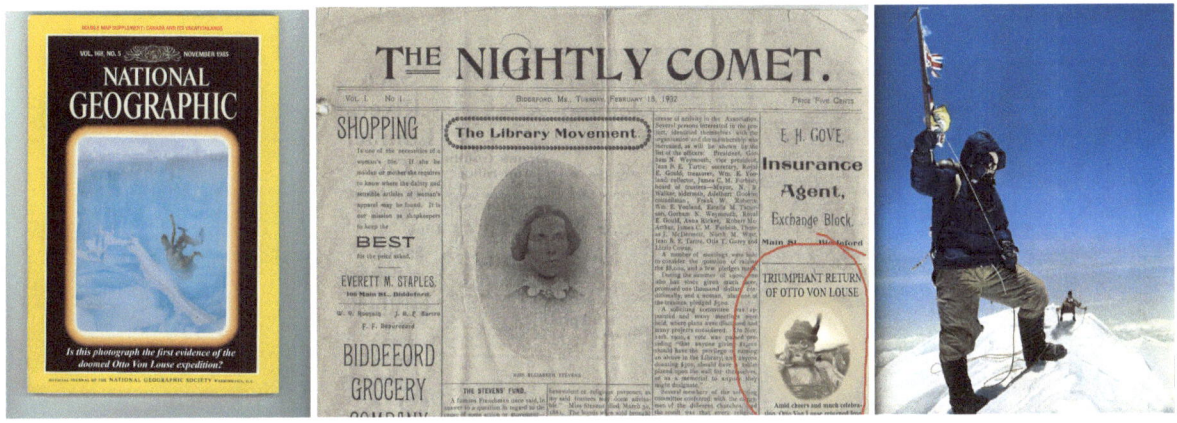

Neil then created a plethora of giveaway items that could be used during promotional and fund-raising efforts, such as KickStarter.

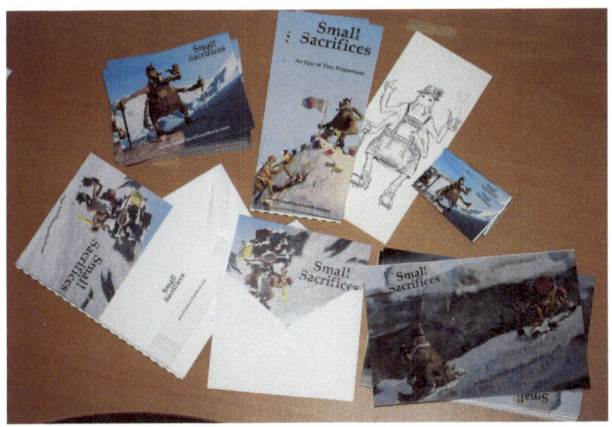

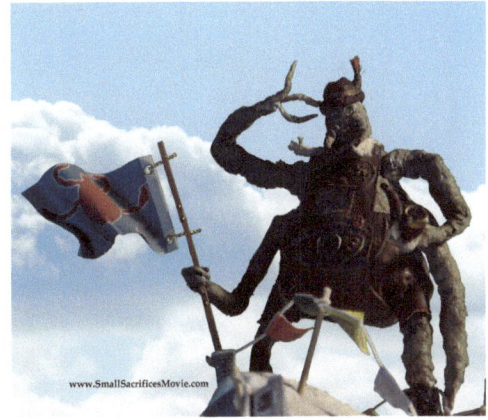

Alongside these promotional items, Neil also developed a website with Patrick Stallard, which echoed the period feel of the film

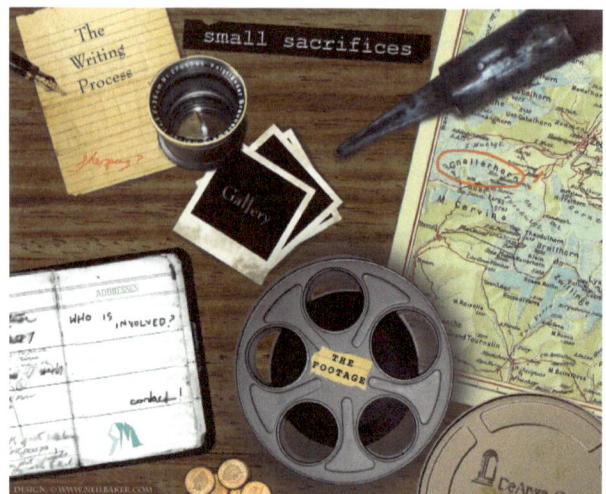 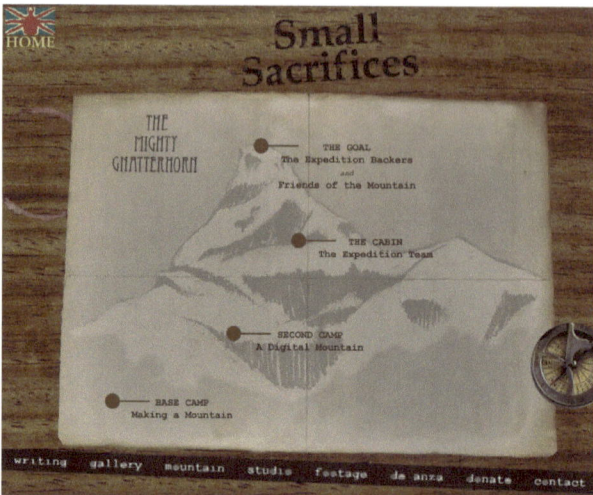

Neil also collaborated with Phil to create an official poster for the film. His only mandate was that it should look like an old Drew Struzen type poster with floating scenes and dynamic composition. Once again, Phil delivered.

Phil's rough sketch of the poster   The final image

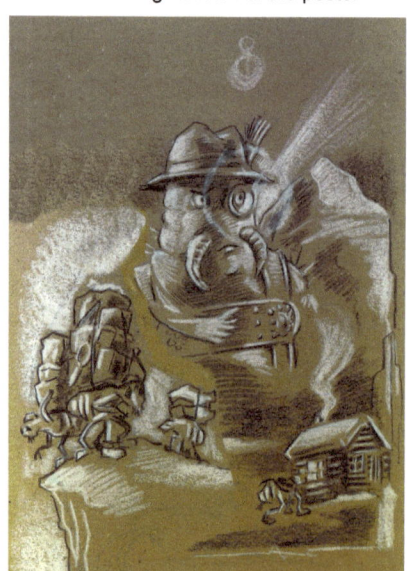 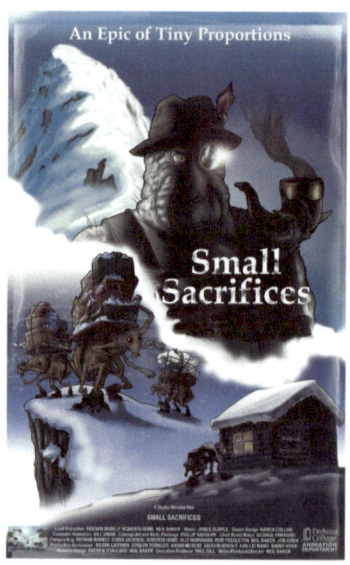

Credits

Neil Baker   Keenan Manely   Roberta Home   Bill Dwan   James Semple   Karen Collins   Phillip Vaughan

George Parashis   Jon Oren   Chris Jackson   Rob Pendleton   Alix Herrmann   Naomi Meyers   Eileen Laitinen

Joel Natanauan   Jimmy Phan   Jacob Rossi   Mario Hsieh   Han-Lei Wang   Paul Gill

Many Thanks

Martin McNamara   Dave Perry   Kuldip Gill   Tom Schott   Tim Canale

Dennis Irwin   Susan Tavernetti   Tim Taylor   Zaki Lisha

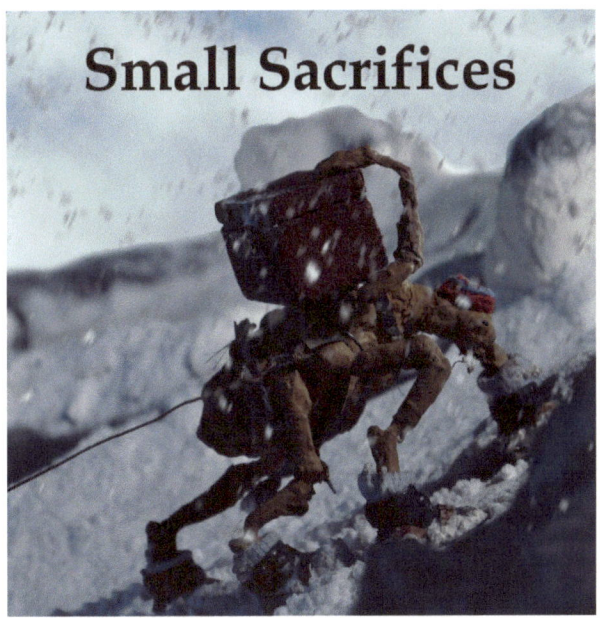

At the time of going to press *Small Sacrifices* is still a work in progress, and the filmmakers intend to present the finished film at festivals worldwide in the coming months and years. Thank you for your support.